# Accidental Scientific Discoveries That Changed the World

# OOPS! THEY'RE X-RAYS!

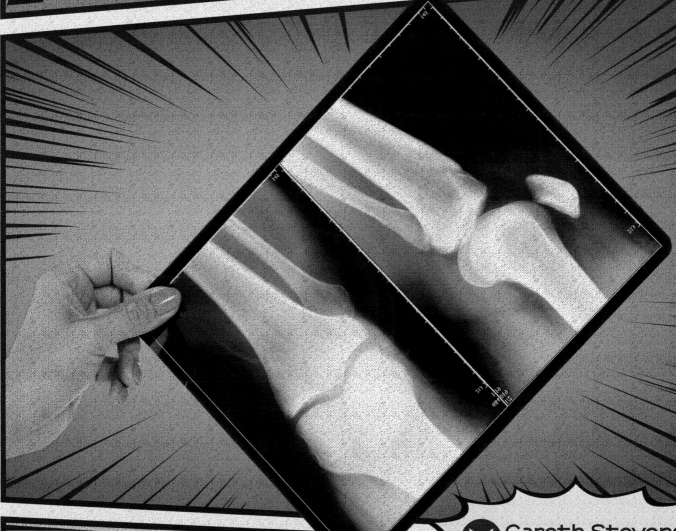

BY NICK WOJTON

Gareth Stevens
PUBLISHING

**Please visit our website, www.garethstevens.com. For a free color catalog of all our high-quality books, call toll free 1-800-542-2595 or fax 1-877-542-2596.**

**Library of Congress Cataloging-in-Publication Data**

Names: Wojton, Nick, author.
Title: Oops! They're x-rays! / Nick Wojton.
Other titles: Oops! They are x-rays
Description: New York : Gareth Stevens Publishing, [2020] | Series:
  Accidental scientific discoveries that changed the world | Includes
  bibliographical references and index.
Identifiers: LCCN 2018057053| ISBN 9781538240021 (pbk.) | ISBN 9781538240045
  (library bound) | ISBN 9781538240038 (6 pack)
Subjects: LCSH: R?ontgen, Wilhelm Conrad, 1845-1923–Juvenile literature. |
  X-rays–Juvenile literature. | Radiography–Juvenile literature. |
  Discoveries in science–Juvenile literature.
Classification: LCC RC78 .W5975 2020 | DDC 539.7/222–dc23
LC record available at https://lccn.loc.gov/2018057053

First Edition

Published in 2020 by
**Gareth Stevens Publishing**
111 East 14th Street, Suite 349
New York, NY 10003

Copyright © 2020 Gareth Stevens Publishing

Designer: Katelyn E. Reynolds
Editor: Monika Davies

Photo credits: Cover, p. 1 Dmitry Lobanov/Shutterstock.com; cover, pp. 1–32 (burst) jirawat phueksriphan/
Shutterstock.com; cover, pp. 1–32 (burst lines) KID_A/Shutterstock.com; p. 5 alessandro guerriero/
Shutterstock.com; p. 7 VectorMine/Shutterstock.com; p. 9 kaling2100/Shutterstock.com; p. 11 ETH-Bibliothek/
Wikipedia.org; p. 13 D-Kuru/Wikipedia.org; p. 15 Deutsches Röntgen-Museum (https://web.archive.org/
web/20160915155603/https://www.roentgen-museum.de/fileadmin/bilder_inhalte/DRM_DL_Labor
Roentgen.jpg)/Drdoht/Wikipedia.org; p. 17 E rulez/Jarekt/Wikipedia.org; p. 19 SSPL/Getty Images;
p. 21 Universal History Archive / UIG via Getty Images; p. 25 Tyler Olson/Shutterstock.com; p. 27 Dreams
Come True/Shutterstock.com; p. 29 courtesy of NASA.

Printed in the United States of America

CPSIA compliance information: Batch #CS19GS: For further information contact Gareth Stevens, New York, New York at 1-800-542-2595.

# CONTENTS

Words in the glossary appear in **bold** type the first time they are used in the text.

# PHOTOGRAPHING OUR INSIDES

Imagine trying to fix something without being able to see exactly what's wrong. Before 1895, if you broke a bone in your body, doctors had no way of seeing inside your body to see where the break was. Doctors had to cut into flesh to "see" inside to fix the problem.

Now, X-ray machines can take photographs of the inside of your body. This is an important tool in the medical world. However, even though various X-ray machines are now used around the world, no one set out to invent the original machine. The discovery of X-rays was an accident!

# METHOD OR IMAGE? BOTH!

WE USE THE WORD X-RAY IN A VARIETY OF WAYS. X-RAYS ARE A TYPE OF ENERGY WAVE. BUT, YOU CAN ALSO SAY YOU'RE GETTING AN X-RAY, WHICH MEANS THE METHOD OF USING X-RAYS TO TAKE AN IMAGE OF THE INSIDE OF YOUR BODY. AND, AN X-RAY CAN ALSO MEAN THE ACTUAL IMAGE OF THE INSIDE OF THE BODY.

X-ray machines allow us to take quick, pain-free pictures of the inside of our bodies. This helps medical professionals figure out the best way to treat someone's illness or injury.

5

# UNDERSTANDING X-RAYS

X-rays are a type of electromagnetic **radiation**. These are energy waves that are part electric and part magnetic. X-rays are a powerful kind of energy, like light is, but are **invisible** to the human eye.

These invisible waves are placed on a **spectrum** with other kinds of electromagnetic radiation. There are seven types of electromagnetic radiation: radio, microwave, infrared, visible light, ultraviolet, X-rays, and gamma rays. Waves of energy are named based on their wavelength, or the amount of space between one energy wave and the next. X-rays have a very small wavelength compared to other waves of energy.

# THE SMALLER, THE STRONGER

AS A WAVELENGTH GETS SMALLER, IT BECOMES STRONGER. SHORT WAVELENGTHS HAVE MORE ENERGY. X-RAYS HAVE ONE OF THE SHORTEST WAVELENGTHS ON THE ELECTROMAGNETIC SPECTRUM, SO THEY HAVE HIGHER ENERGY THAN OTHER WAVELENGTHS. THESE POWERFUL X-RAYS ARE ABLE TO EASILY PENETRATE, OR GO THROUGH, MANY KINDS OF MATTER.

Each type of electromagnetic radiation has a different sized wavelength. X-rays have the second-shortest wavelength.

## THE SEVEN TYPES OF ELECTROMAGNETIC RADIATION

| RADIO | MICROWAVES | INFRARED | VISIBLE LIGHT | ULTRAVIOLET | X-RAYS | GAMMA |
|-------|------------|----------|---------------|-------------|--------|-------|

7

Your body is made of skin, muscle, **tissue**, and bone. Each of these have a different density, or amount of a matter in a certain area. X-rays have a high energy and can pass easily through less dense materials, like your skin, muscle, and tissue.

However, X-rays can't pass through bone. Since X-rays can't travel through bone, we can use them to create images of the human skeleton. X-ray machines make these images. In an X-ray machine, X-rays pass through the body and hit an X-ray **detector**, which can create a black-and-white image of the inside of the body.

# On the Job

X-RAYS HAVE BECOME VERY IMPORTANT IN THE MEDICAL WORLD. THERE IS EVEN A JOB THAT DEALS DIRECTLY WITH X-RAYS! AN X-RAY TECHNICIAN IS SOMEONE WHO HAS SPECIAL TRAINING IN USING X-RAY MACHINES. THEY CAN HELP DOCTORS TO SEE IF SOMETHING IS WRONG!

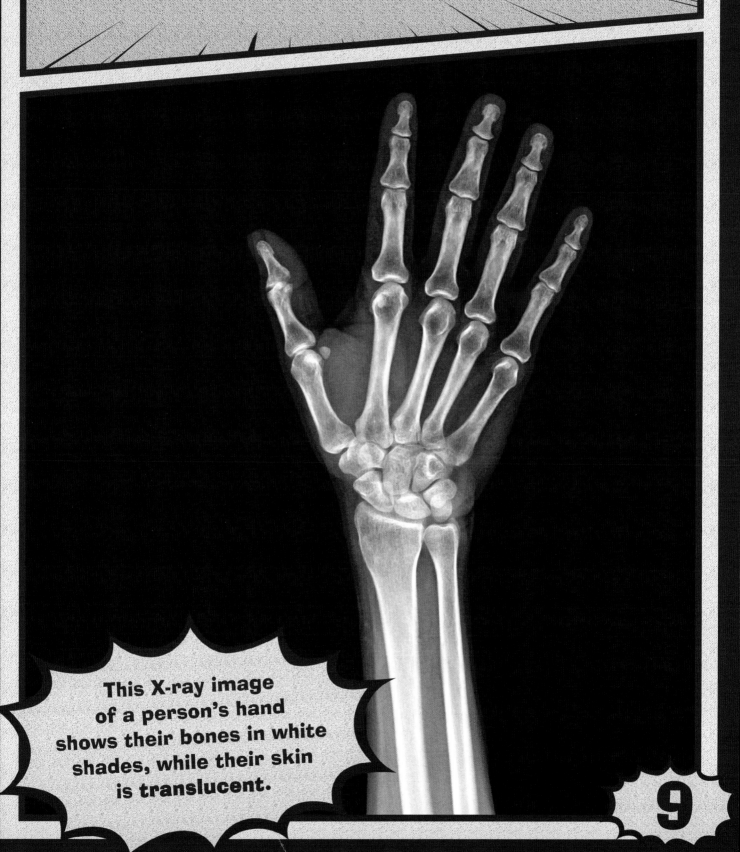

This X-ray image of a person's hand shows their bones in white shades, while their skin is translucent.

9

# DISCOVERING X-RAYS

German scientist Wilhelm Röntgen was working in his laboratory in Würzburg, Germany, when he chanced upon a big discovery. Röntgen was an **expert** in physics, or the study of matter, energy, force, and motion, and the relationship among them. He taught physics at several German universities during his lifetime.

Röntgen often worked on experiments. He examined and tested how different gases, fluids, and crystals reacted, or changed, after coming in contact with a certain kind of matter. On November 8, 1895, Röntgen was experimenting with a Crookes tube. This is a glass tube shaped like a flower vase but closed at both ends.

# Wilhelm Röntgen

Wilhelm Röntgen's discovery of x-rays made a huge difference in the medical community. He earned many awards and prize money for his discovery. However, he was a modest person and never tried to profit, or make money, from his discovery. Röntgen ended up giving all his prize money to one of the universities where he worked.

Wilhelm Röntgen liked to work alone when he was experimenting. He often built his own equipment for his scientific tests.

11

At the time, scientists understood when electricity passed through the Crookes tube, this created cathode rays. These rays are beams of electrons, or **particles** found in atoms that act as a carrier of electricity in solids. Cathode rays are a type of radiation, or waves of energy.

Röntgen was experimenting with the Crookes tube to learn more about cathode rays. He was interested in seeing how far they'd travel. While looking over the tube, Röntgen noticed that a chemical-covered board from another experiment began glowing across the room. This happened even when the Crookes tube was covered with black cardboard!

# THE FIRST NOBEL PRIZE WINNER

THE NOBEL PRIZE IS AWARDED TO PEOPLE WHO MAKE DISCOVERIES THAT HELP HUMANS. IN 1901, WILHELM RÖNTGEN WAS THE FIRST TO BE AWARDED THE NOBEL PRIZE IN PHYSICS FOR HIS DISCOVERY OF X-RAYS. ALBERT EINSTEIN IS ONE OF THE MOST FAMOUS PHYSICISTS TO WIN THE NOBEL PRIZE.

English scientist Sir William Crookes invented the Crookes tube in the 1870s. He used it to study different kinds of gas.

13

Röntgen knew he'd made an important observation. To his knowledge, cathode rays couldn't travel far. So, the cathode rays weren't the reason why the board had begun to glow. Röntgen figured out the tube had to be giving off a different kind of ray. And, this new ray could travel through dark, **opaque** paper.

Röntgen decided to focus his efforts on learning the features of this new ray. He spent 6 weeks experimenting with different kinds of matter. He found the rays could pass through certain matter, like wood and paper. He also discovered these rays, when directed at certain matter, could make an image of shadows on a photographic plate.

# BEHIND THE NAME

UPON HIS DISCOVERY OF X-RAYS, RÖNTGEN STARTED WRITING DOWN EVERYTHING HE LEARNED. HE DIDN'T FULLY UNDERSTAND WHAT X-RAYS WERE MADE OF, SO HE CALLED THEM AN "UNKNOWN" RAY. IN MATHEMATICS, "X" REPRESENTS AN "UNKNOWN." SO, THESE UNKNOWN RAYS BECAME KNOWN AS "X-RAYS." HOWEVER, SOME PEOPLE STILL CALL THEM RÖNTGEN RAYS FOR THE PHYSICIST!

Röntgen was asked what his first thoughts were when he discovered X-rays. He replied, "I didn't think, I investigated." This is the laboratory where he spent his time experimenting and investigating.

Röntgen continued experimenting. One day, he realized that if he placed his hand in front of a path of X-rays headed toward a screen, his bones appeared as dark shadows on the screen. However, his skin appeared as a lighter gray color. He realized X-rays could travel through skin and tissue but not through bones.

This was a big discovery. Röntgen asked his wife, Bertha, to place her hand upon a photographic plate. He then aimed X-rays at her hand. One of the first X-ray images is of her hand, which shows her bones—as well as her metal wedding ring. Röntgen had found a way to look inside the human body!

# METAL BARRIERS

X-RAYS HAVE A HIGH ENERGY, SO THEY CAN PASS THROUGH MOST OBJECTS. HOWEVER, X-RAYS CAN'T PASS THROUGH METAL OBJECTS, LIKE ZIPPERS OR RINGS. IF YOU GO FOR AN X-RAY, THE TECHNICIAN MAY ASK YOU TO REMOVE ANY METAL YOU'RE WEARING TO MAKE SURE THEY CAN TAKE A CLEAR PICTURE.

Röntgen took this early X-ray image of Albert von Kölliker's hand.

# POPULAR FROM THE BEGINNING

Röntgen took his time to discover the true power of X-rays in his laboratory in Germany. In December 1895, he published a paper titled "On A New Kind of Rays."

Word spread fast about Röntgen's discovery. Scientists around the world began using X-rays to take images. On February 3, 1896, Edwin Frost took an X-ray image of a young boy's broken wrist in Dartmouth, Massachusetts. This was the first medical X-ray image taken. Soon, X-ray machines were used more and more to **diagnose** problems inside the body. Less than a year later, the first X-ray department in a hospital was established in Glasgow, Scotland.

# MARIE CURIE'S RADIOLOGICAL CAR

X-RAY MACHINES BECAME AN IMPORTANT TOOL DURING TIMES OF WAR. THEY BECAME KEY TO HELPING DOCTORS IDENTIFY THE INJURIES OF SOLDIERS. IN 1914, MARIE CURIE, A WELL-KNOWN SCIENTIST, CREATED ONE OF THE FIRST CARS FOR CARRYING X-RAY MACHINES OUT ONTO THE BATTLEFIELD. THESE CARS WERE KNOWN AS "LITTLE CURIES"!

This glass tube produces X-rays and releases them through the glass.

19

Röntgen's discovery of X-rays changed the medical world. For certain problems inside the body, doctors could now see what the issue might be without cutting open the body. However, while X-rays were used for serious purposes, X-rays also originally had some fun uses.

Shortly after the discovery of X-rays, they began appearing in cartoons and short stories. X-ray machines were featured at fairs and carnivals. Places popped up where X-ray machines took "bone portraits" of people. X-rays were even used to take pictures of people's feet in stores to figure out their shoe size!

# Presidential Save

IN 1881, US PRESIDENT JAMES GARFIELD DIED AFTER HE WAS SHOT. HIS DOCTORS COULDN'T FIND THE BULLET IN GARFIELD TO SAVE HIS LIFE. A CENTURY LATER IN 1981, PRESIDENT RONALD REAGAN WAS ALSO SHOT. BUT, WITH THE HELP OF AN X-RAY MACHINE, THE BULLET WAS LOCATED AND SAFELY REMOVED.

X-rays were used for many fun purposes when they were first discovered. However, scientists later learned the dangers of too much exposure to X-ray radiation. Now, the use of X-rays is more regulated, or controlled.

# X-RAY EVOLUTION

X-ray machines have changed since they were created. At first, an X-ray machine was similar to a Crookes tube. It was a glass **cylinder** that sent out X-ray waves toward an item or body part, such as a hand. A photographic plate was set behind the tube, which then captured the X-ray image.

Now, over 100 years after the first X-ray machines were invented, they have a very different appearance. An X-ray machine now looks like a large tube with a light, similar to a camera, that is attached to a wall or ceiling. Most X-ray images are also now electronic files that can be sent and processed as data on computers.

# COOLIDGE X-RAY TUBE

IN 1913, WILLIAM COOLIDGE MADE THE FIRST COOLIDGE X-RAY TUBE. THE TUBE IS STILL WIDELY USED TODAY. IT CONTAINED A HEATED CATHODE FILAMENT, OR THIN-THREADLIKE OBJECT, THAT PRODUCES ELECTRONS. THESE ELECTRONS HIT THE TUBE'S **ANODE**, CREATING X-RAYS. THIS BEAM OF X-RAYS WAS STEADY AND COULD BE EASILY CHANGED TO FIT THE USER'S NEEDS.

X-ray tubes are kept in a thick case with a window. The window is where the beam of X-rays is directed outward.

# HOW AN X-RAY MACHINE WORKS

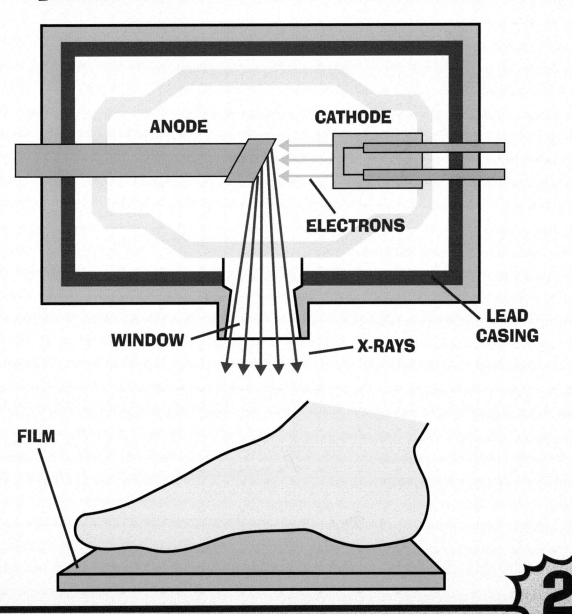

ANODE

CATHODE

ELECTRONS

WINDOW

X-RAYS

LEAD CASING

FILM

# X-TRA USES

X-ray images are best known for identifying where bones are broken. However, X-ray images can also help spot and solve many other medical issues because the images show tissues of different densities in the body.

Chest X-rays are used to see if someone has pneumonia, or a serious illness in the lungs caused by an **infection**. X-rays of the body's midsection can tell if someone has kidney problems. X-rays are also used to see if someone has a tumor, or a mass of tissue with harmful cells. Mammograms use X-rays to see if someone has breast cancer. Dentists also use X-rays to look at your teeth to see if you have cavities, or holes in your teeth.

# CT Scans

THE COMPUTED TOMOGRAPHY SCANNER (CT SCAN) IS A VERSION OF THE X-RAY MACHINE THAT USES COMPUTER TECHNOLOGY. A CT SCAN SENDS X-RAYS FROM MULTIPLE DIRECTIONS INTO YOUR BODY. THE MACHINE RECORDS HOW FAR THE X-RAYS TRAVEL, SENDING THAT INFORMATION TO A COMPUTER. THE COMPUTER THEN PRODUCES A MORE DEVELOPED, 360-DEGREE IMAGE OF THE INSIDE OF YOUR BODY.

Godfrey Hounsfield built the first CT scanner in 1971. It took pictures of the brain.

25

# OUCH!

Soon after the discovery of X-rays, scientists began worrying about the side effects of X-ray radiation. It's now known that certain types of radiation can cause **nausea** and burns. A large amount of radiation can lead to more serious illnesses such as cancer.

However, getting an X-ray is now very safe. In 1968, the United States passed the Radiation Control for Health and Safety Act. This made sure X-ray machines could only emit, or give off, a certain amount of radiation. We are also exposed to X-rays for less time now. The first X-ray machines took around 90 minutes to take a picture. Today, an X-ray machine can take a picture in 20 milliseconds!

# Too Strong

RADIATION CAN HARM LIVING TISSUE. THE ORIGINAL X-RAY MACHINES EXPOSED PEOPLE TO DANGEROUS LEVELS OF RADIATION. THESE MACHINES EXPOSED PEOPLE TO 1,500 TIMES MORE RADIATION THAN A MODERN-DAY X-RAY MACHINE! X-RAY MACHINES NOW GIVE OFF A LOT LESS RADIATION AND ARE A LOT SAFER TO USE.

If you get an X-ray now, you might wear a lead apron. This helps protect you from radiation's side effects since X-rays can't pass through lead.

LEAD APRON

# X-TREMELY IMPORTANT X-RAYS

The discovery of X-rays made a big impact in the medical field. Using X-rays to see inside people has helped save countless lives. But X-rays help us in our day-to-day lives, too.

X-ray machines are commonly used in airport security. When traveling by plane, your baggage is scanned, or viewed, using an X-ray machine. Paintings are often studied with X-rays so art historians can learn more about the history of the artwork. X-rays can reveal the materials and methods the artist used. Röntgen's accidental discovery of X-rays turned out to be an important finding that still helps us in many ways!

# CANCER KILLER

WHILE RADIATION FROM X-RAYS IS KNOWN TO SOMETIMES CAUSE CANCER, IT'S ALSO BEEN USED TO KILL CANCER CELLS! X-RAYS ARE AIMED AT CANCEROUS CELLS AND THE X-RAYS HARM THE CELLS, WHICH STOPS THEM FROM GROWING. THIS IS COMMONLY KNOWN AS RADIATION THERAPY.

The Chandra X-ray Observatory is a telescope that can locate X-rays given off by really hot areas in the solar system. Scientists use the telescope to study black holes, comets, and more.

# GLOSSARY

**anode:** the part of an electrical tool from which electrons exit

**cylinder:** an object shaped like a tube

**detector:** a device that can tell if a certain kind of matter or object is present

**diagnose:** to recognize an illness or injury by examining someone

**expert:** someone who knows a great deal about something

**infection:** a sickness caused by germs

**investigate:** to begin an ordered search for facts about something

**invisible:** unable to be seen

**nausea:** a feeling in the stomach like you're going to throw up

**opaque:** does not let light through

**particle:** a very small piece of something

**radiation:** waves of energy

**spectrum:** range of wavelengths

**tissue:** matter that forms the parts of living things

**translucent:** allowing light to pass through

# FOR MORE INFORMATION

## BOOKS

Canavan, Thomas. *Why Do X-Rays Show Your Bones?: Questions About Bones and Structures.* New York, NY: PowerKids Press, 2017.

Davies, Kate. *Illumanatomy: See Inside the Human Body with your Magic Viewing Lens.* London, UK: Wide Eyed Editions, 2017.

Veasey, Nick. *X-Treme X-Ray: See the World Inside Out!.* New York, NY: Scholastic Books, 2010.

## WEBSITES

### The Electromagnetic Spectrum
*imagine.gsfc.nasa.gov/science/toolbox/emspectrum1.html*
Learn more about the electromagnetic spectrum.

### What Are X-Rays?
*mocomi.com/x-rays/*
Find out more about the science behind X-rays and X-ray machines.

# INDEX